The 'Parents' Time Off' Series

KIDS' GARDENING ACTIVITIES

Geoff Egan
Illustrated by Christine Eddy

Edited by Cecilia Egan

First published in 1990 by Ashton Egan
as The Kids' First Book of Gardening Activities

Revised and updated 2015
Copyright © Leaves of Gold Press 2015
The right of Geoff Egan to be identified as author of this work has been
asserted in accordance with the Copyright, Designs and Patents Act, 1988.

National Library of Australia Cataloguing-in-Publication entry

Creator: Egan, Geoff, author.

Title: Kids' gardening activities / Geoff Egan ;

Christine Eddy, illustrator.

Cecilia Egan, editor

Edition: 2nd edition

ISBN: 9781925110692 (paperback)

Series: Parents' time off series ; 2.

Target Audience: For primary school age (6-12 year old)

Subjects: Gardening--Juvenile literature.

Other Creators/Contributors:

Eddy, Christine, illustrator.

Dewey Number: 635.048

LEAVES of GOLD PRESS

ABN 67 099 575 078

PO Box 9113, Brighton, 3186, Victoria, Australia
www.leavesofgoldpress.com

INTRODUCTION

Kids' Gardening Activities contains fun gardening projects for young children to enjoy. Any child from six to twelve years old can undertake these activities. However, it might be worth noting the three gradings:

Activities are graded with star symbols:
* Very easy
** Easy
*** An adult's help might be needed

This book does not aim to be a gardening manual, but rather a book to introduce children to gardening in a fun way. We hope that with such an introduction, gardening will remain a life-long joy.

CONTENTS

LEAF SHAPES*

Try to find as many different types of leaves
as you can. Choose thin, flat leaves.

Crenate

Linear

Ovate

Trifoliate

Lobed

Needle

Pinnate

Palmate

Leaf hunting in
autumn is great fun
because of the
varieties of
colours and
shapes that
can be
collected.

Liquidambar leaf

1

LEAF PRESSING *

Place collected leaves between two sheets of absorbent paper.
Find a heavy book. Put the leaves inside, and close the book. You can also put a weight, such as a stone, on top of the book to keep the leaves flat.

Keep the book somewhere dry. After a week, check the leaves and throw out any rotten ones. Leave the leaves inside the book for another 1-2 weeks until they have completely dried out.

Fold

Use pressed leaves to decorate cards and stationery, or arrange them on paper to make a pretty wall decoration,

SEED COLLECTION*

See if you can find some seed pods to collect.

Pomegranate

Acorn

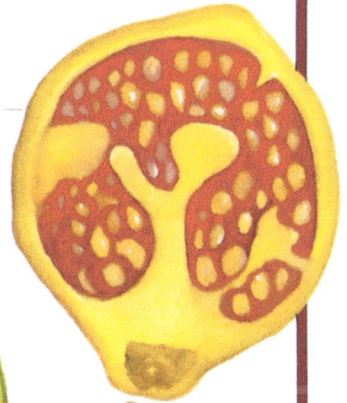

Poppy

Hakea

Pinecone

1. Look around in parks, coastal reserves, woodlands, forests and your own garden.
Some will have seeds still inside.
Others will have released their seeds, leaving only the woody seed-cases — ideal for spraying with gold or silver paint for decorations!

2. Put your seed-filled pods into a paper bag and hang them to dry in a warm place. They will release the seeds when they dry out.

4. Plant the seeds immediately, or if you want to plant them later, store your seeds in a cool, dry place such as the refrigerator.

LEAF CREATURES*

Go on a leaf-creature search.

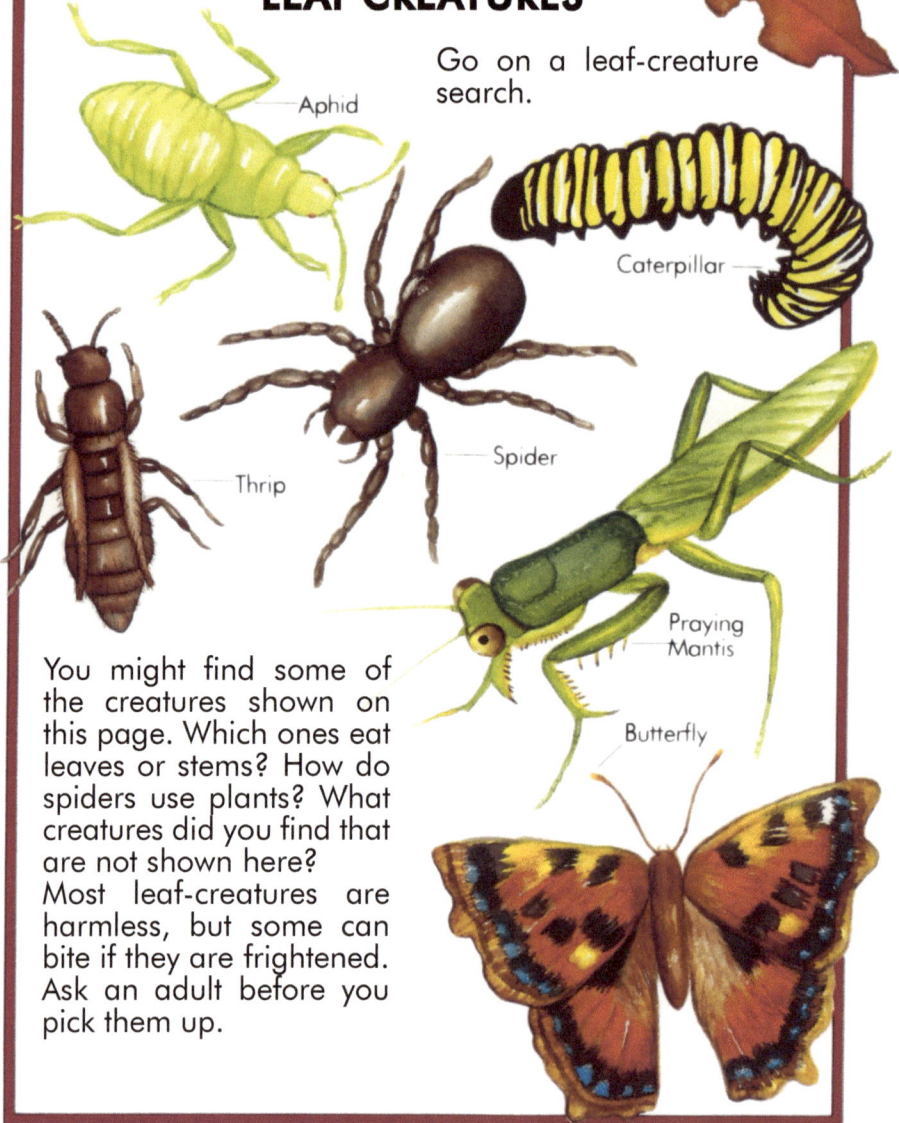

Aphid

Caterpillar

Spider

Thrip

Praying Mantis

Butterfly

You might find some of the creatures shown on this page. Which ones eat leaves or stems? How do spiders use plants? What creatures did you find that are not shown here?

Most leaf-creatures are harmless, but some can bite if they are frightened. Ask an adult before you pick them up.

SOIL CREATURES*

Ant

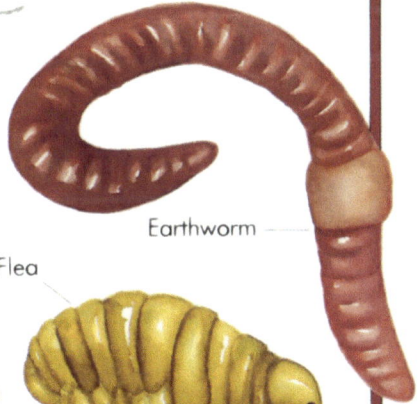

Earthworm

Flea

Slater

In backyards tiny creatures may hide underneath up-turned flower-pots, sticks, bricks, or fallen leaves.

Make sure there are holes in container

Springtail

Can you find any?
Take some of your creatures to school and find out what they eat. Be kind to them.
Release the creatures back into their homes after a day or two.

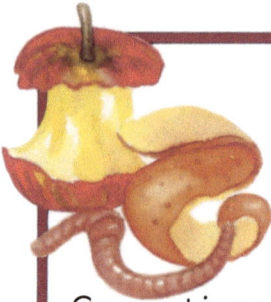

COMPOST HEAP*

It is important for gardens to have a healthy compost heap.

Compost is a mixture of stuff that has once been alive ('organic matter)', and which has been allowed to rot. When it rots it turns into a fertilizer for growing plants. Organic kitchen waste such as vegetable peelings, fruit cores, tea leaves and food scraps can be placed in a combost bin or a compost bay.

Lawn clippings and fallen leaves from your garden can be added to your compost. When you've built up a layer of scraps, top them with a layer of soil from your garden before adding the next layer of scraps. Water your compost heap during dry spells.

It will take about six months for the kitchen and garden scraps to break down and become proper compost. When it is ready, dig the compost in to your garden beds. Plants love it!

HINT: To help the scraps break down faster, cover your compost heap with a sheet of plastic.

INDOOR
CARROT FOREST*

1. Find a shallow bowl and fill it with gravel. Add enough water to come up to the top of the gravel.

2. Cut the tops off some carrots. Try to select carrots that have some new shoots.

3. Place the carrot tops on the moist gravel and put the container in a sunny position. A window sill is ideal.

4. Keep gravel moist and watch your carrot 'trees' grow.

NOTE: Because there is no soil to provide food, after a while the carrot 'trees' will die. If you want to grow new carrots, plant carrot seeds in your garden.

INDOOR WHEAT GARDEN*

1. Find a shallow, wide bowl and line it with a thick layer of cotton wool.

2. Pour cool, clean water onto the cotton wool to make it moist, but not soaking wet.

3. Place a handful of wheat on top of the moist cotton wool. You can buy wheat from some health food stores, or from stores that sell food for horses and birds.

4. Watch your wheat 'germinate'. The wheat seeds will sprout and grow into green blades, like grass.

NOTE: Instead of wheat, you could use bird seed.

DIVIDING
A BEGONIA PLANT*

Begonia plants can be grown indoors. Grow them outdoors if you live in a warm climate. To make two plants out of one, divide it.

1. Using a small trowel, split the plant down the middle.

2. Make sure you keep all the roots. One half can be transplanted into another pot or a a different part of your garden.
Water it well.

3. The remaining half will grow and flourish in its orginal location.

GROW NEW PLANTS
FROM CUTTINGS**

1. Some plants can be grown from cuttings. We have chosen a pelargonium plant (sometimes called a geranium).

Others that grow easily from cuttings include African violets, Coleus, Impatiens and Philodendrons.

2. Using secateurs (be careful), cut off a stem from the mother plant. Make the cut just below a place where a leaf joins the stem.

3. Remove a few leaves from the base of the stem.

4. Also remove any flowers or buds. This is because the new plant will need to put its energy into growing new roots, instead of growing flowers and buds.

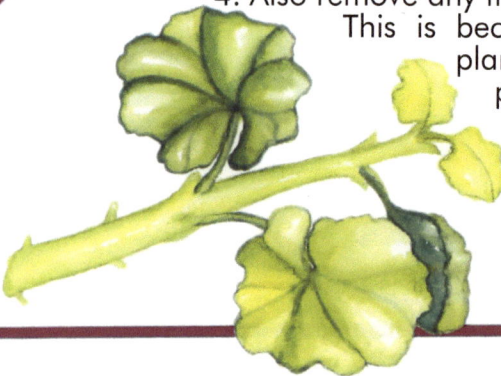

5. In a bucket, mix together equal quantities of clean river sand and potting mix. Or, use ready-made 'propagating mix'. You can buy all these from plant nurseries.

Wrong

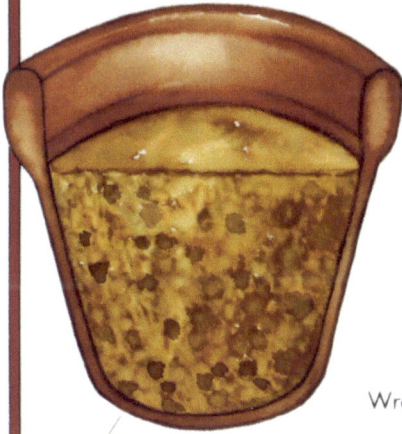

Make sure there are no air pockets

6. Put your soil mixture into a plant pot. Do not fill the pot to the top edge, because when you water it, the water would run off. Leave about 25 millimetres (1 inch).

7. Make a hole in the soil mixture with a stick or your finger. Put the cutting into the hole.

8. Place the pot in a sunny spot (but not too hot!) and water it every 2-3 days. After a few weeks the cutting will have grown roots and you will have made a new plant!

Make sure plant stem does not touch the bottom of pot

PEPEROMIA
LEAF CUTTINGS**

Peperomia plants have lots of different, pretty leaf shapes, and grow easily from leaf cuttings.

1.   Place some propagating soil mix (or river sand mixed with potting mix) into a plant pot. Note that plant pots have drainage holes in the bottom.

2. Using secateurs or scissors, remove some leaves from the mother plant. Cut close to the base of the mother plant without damaging it.

3. Make some holes in the soil mix with a stick.

4. Put leaves in the holes without breaking the stems.

5. Keep the soil moist and the pot in a sunny spot. After a couple of weeks, you will see the shoots of your new plant.

Peperomia plants grow well indoors, near a window.

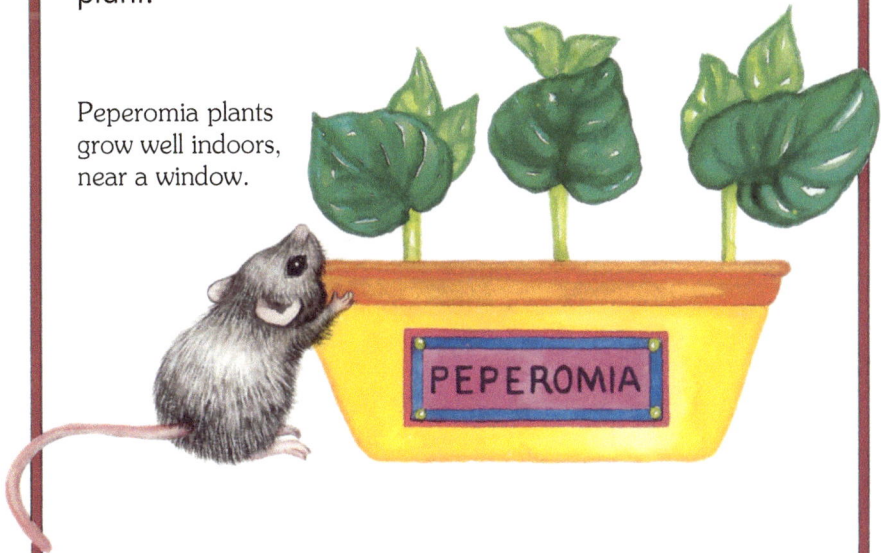

PEPEROMIA

GROWING A PLANT IN WATER*
The Piggy-Back Plant

Cut here

The Piggy-Back Plant's scientific name is *Tolmiea menziesii*. It can be grown indoors.

1. Remove a leaf from the mother plant — make sure you cut at the base of the leaf.

2. Three quarters fill a jar with water.

3. Cover the top of the jar with a piece of plastic food-wrap or other soft plastic sheeting, and secure it in place with an elastic band.

4. Prick a hole in the plastic and poke the leaf-stem through until the stem is under the water.

5. Leave the jar near a window but not in direct sunlight. If the water level drops below the stem, top it up with more water.

6. After 2 - 3 weeks, roots will start to appear. When your plant has lots of roots, plant it in a pot of potting mix.

LAYERING AZALEAS **
to make a new plant

An easy way of creating a new plant is by layering.

1. Find a bush with low-growing branches. Azaleas are ideal.

2. Loosen the soil at Point A and bury the stem under the ground. Pin the branch so that it does not pop up. Use a piece of wire bent into a U-shape.

3. Be patient. It can take several months for roots to start sprouting from the buried section.

4. After roots form, trim off the branch at Point B.

A

The newly separated piece with its own roots is a new plant!

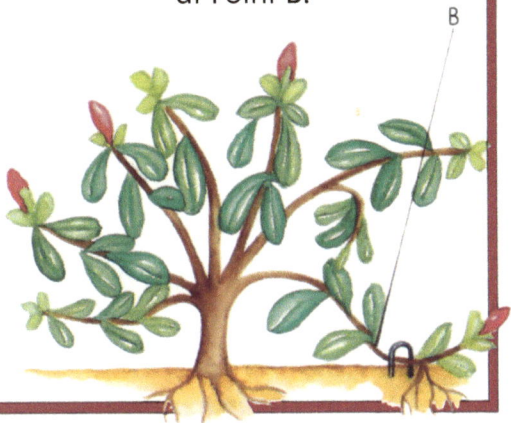

B

HERBS — PARSLEY *

Parsley is an ideal plant to grow in a pot. It is also delicious to eat - and good for you!

Plant parsley seeds or seedlings in a good potting mix and water them regularly. Keep the pot outdoors, or if you live in a cold climate, grow parsley on a sunny windowsill.
Use parsley as a garnish to decorate food, or make tasty tabouli salad.

HERBS — CHIVES*

Another easy-to-grow and delicious herb is chives. Grow them in a pot in well-drained soil. Water them well and keep them in a sunny position.
If you grow chives in summer you can chop them into salads. In winter you can use them to bake savory muffins.

AVOCADO PLANT **

You can grow an attractive plant from the seed inside an avocado.

1. Stick four toothpicks into the avocado stone.

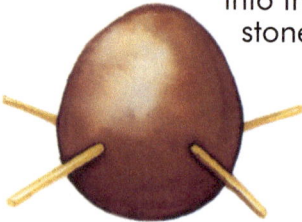

2. Then put the stone into a glass filled with water, larger end downwards.

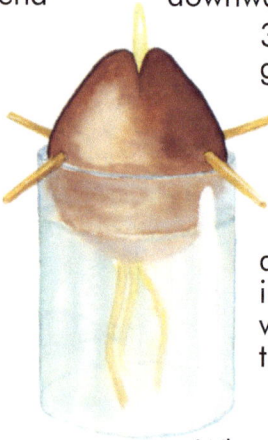

3. Keep the glass filled ith water and roots should appear in about five weeks.

4. Plant your avocado stone into a pot and watch your tree grow!

When it's bigger you might have to transfer it to a larger pot or plant it in the garden.

POTATO PLANTS **

From one potato we can grow many potato plants.

1. Wait until the potato starts to shoot.

2. Cut the potato into sections. Get an adult to help!
Make sure each section has an 'eye' or a shoot.

3. Store these segments for 2 - 3 days in a warm place.

4. Plant segments into the soil, about 10 cm (4 inches) deep and 20 - 25 cm (8 - 10 inches) apart. This gives them enough space to grow.

Each piece will become a new potato plant!

POTATOES

SEED SOWING**

Make sure you sow your seeds at the right time of year. Read the instructions on the seed packet to find out when.

1. Find a large, shallow container with drainage holes. Fill it 3/4 full with a light potting mix, such as 'seed raising mix'.

2. Level off the soil so that it's flat and not bumpy.

3. Spread smaller seeds such as carrot or tomato evenly over the top of the soil. Larger seeds, such as pumpkin, can be pushed into the soil at equal intervals.

Seeds should be planted at a depth of three times the thickness of the seed.

4. Sprinkle a layer of soil over your seeds. You could use a sieve to make sure there are no lumps.

Wet the soil with a fine spray of water.
Keep the soil moist while the seeds are sprouting.

Old margarine and butter containers can be used as seed-sowing containers.

After your seeds start sprouting, make sure you keep watering them with your sprayer. The fine mist should not dislodge tiny seeds.

Easy seeds to start with are radishes, alyssum, calendula and pumpkin.

Use an ice-cream/popsicle stick to label your seeds.

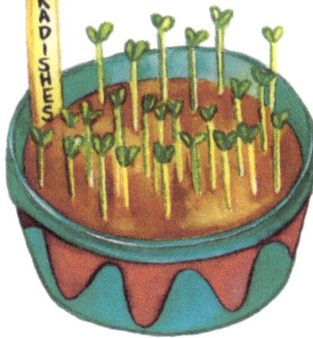

TRANSPLANTING YOUR SEEDLINGS**

When the seeds have outgrown the propagation contaner, you can plant them in a larger container with fewer seedlings, or plant them in the open garden.

1. Make the new soil moist. It must not be lumpy.

2. Water your seeds before transplanting. It is a big event for them and they need moisture to help them survive the move.

3. Make a hole in the ground a little deeper than the seedlings' roots.

4. Insert the seedling and lightly press the soil back into the hole without damaging your plant.

LOOKING AFTER
YOUR SEEDLINGS**

1. Do not make the soil soggy with too much water.

2. If too many seeds sprout and the seedlings are over-crowded, you can thin them out by removing some of them.

Before thinning

After thinning

The remaining seedlings will have more space. They will grow bigger and healthier.

Not enough light

3. Give them a sunny spot. If your seeds are not getting enough sunlight they will look spindly and pale.

Good light

PLANTING A
HANGING BASKET***

1. Either buy a wire hanging basket or make a wooden one out of a box.

Wire

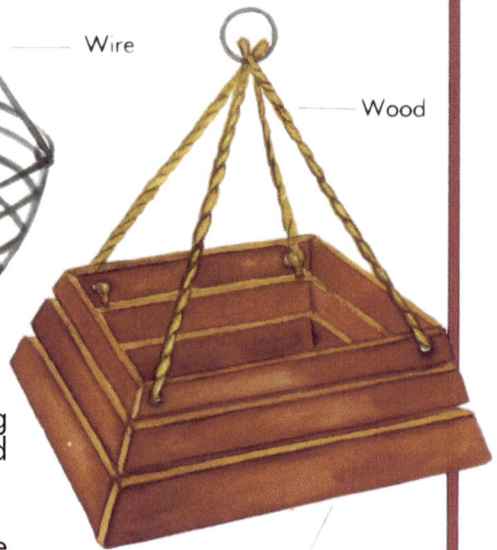

Wood

2. Line your hanging basket with bark or old carpet felt.

If you use bark, line the basket first with heavy-duty plastic sheets. This stops moisture from running out too fast.

Make sure there are no gaps between slats. Put drainage holes in wood.

3. Half fill the basket with potting mix. You can buy this from your local nursery.

4 Set your plant in the middle of the container.

5. Line the surface of the soil with spaghnum moss.

6. Keep your hanging basket away from too much direct heat. Most importantly, keep it moist by watering it regularly, especially in hot weather!

7. Baskets that are hanging high up can be watered with a squeeze container with a long spout.

HAIRY HARRY**

1. Combine some potting mix with a sprinkling of cress seeds, grass seeds or bird seed

2. Cut off the leg of a stocking about 20 cm (8 inches) from the toe.

3. Fill the toe of the stocking with the soil-and-seed mixture. When it is about the size of a tennis ball, tie up the stocking close to the soil lump.

4. Put some water in the bottom of a plastic cup such as an old yoghurt container. Place the filled stocking on top of the cup, letting the loose part trail in the water. Make sure there is always water in the cup.

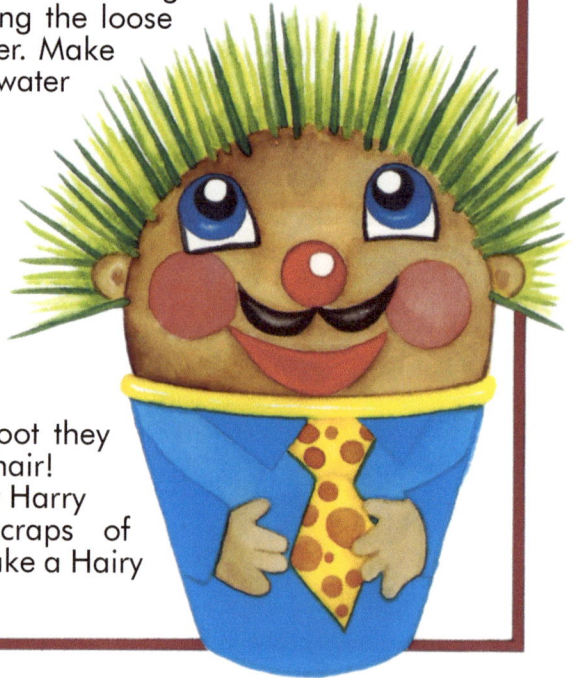

When the seeds shoot they will look like green hair! Decorate your Hairy Harry with paint and scraps of fabric. You could make a Hairy Harry family!

EGG HEAD**

Next time you have a boiled egg to eat, sit the egg in an egg-cup and carefully cut off the top.

Cut

Use a spoon to gently scoop the egg out of the shell. Enjoy eating it!

3. Mix some potting mix with a few pinches of grass seeds.

4. Fill the empty egg shell with the dirt/grass mixture.

5. Keeping it upright in the egg-cup, put it in a warm, sunny place.

6. Water the seeds lightly but do not overwater, because there is no drainage hole at the bottom of the eggshell.

7. Decorate your egg with a funny face. Soon that face will have green hair!

PLASTIC BOTTLE TERRARIUM***

1. Collect a discarded plastic water bottle. We have used a bottle that comes with a black plastic base. If you can't find one, just use a round plastic container for the base. Make sure everything is washed clean!

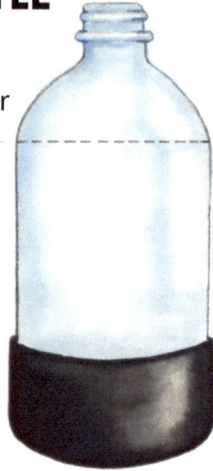

Cut here

Remove

2. Remove the base by soaking it in hot water.

2. Draw a line around the bottle at the place where the neck oins the body.

3. Ask an adult to help you cut the bottle along the line with a pair of scissors. You may need to start a small hole in the bottle before you can cut it.

4. Place a handful of small stones or charcoal at the bottom of the base or the round plastic container.
Then fill it up to the 3/4 mark with potting mix.

Soil level

Charcoal

Drainage

5. Place a small plant into the soil. Crotons, mosses, Pink Polka Dot plant, Golden Pothos and ferns make good terrarium plants.

Do not choose a tall plant because the top of the terrarium will not fit on.

6. Press the plant gently into position and water it lightly.

7. Cover the soil surface with spaghnum moss.

8. Place the plastic dome over the base. This will keep the moisture in, so you should not have to water your terrarium very often.

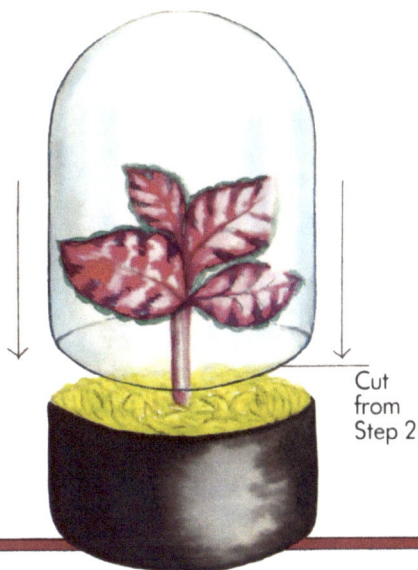

Cut from Step 2

Leaves of Gold Press publishes international, premium quality fiction and non-fiction in hardcover, paperback and ebook format. Our books are printed on high grade, acid-free, book-grade, opaque paper stock sourced from responsibly managed forests.

Our printers are certified by the Forest Stewardship Council™, the Sustainable Forestry Initiative® and the Programme for the Endorsement of Forest Certification™.

Utilizing POD technology reduces paper waste, thereby cutting down greenhouse emissions and conserving valuable natural resources.

LEAVES of GOLD
PRESS
®

The best books for children, young adults and adults.

www.leavesofgoldpress.com

The 'Parents' Time Off' Series

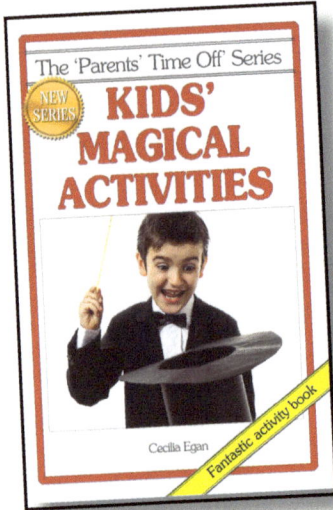

The 'Parents' Time Off' Series

NEW SERIES

KIDS'
MAGICAL
ACTIVITIES

Cecilia Egan

Fantastic activity book

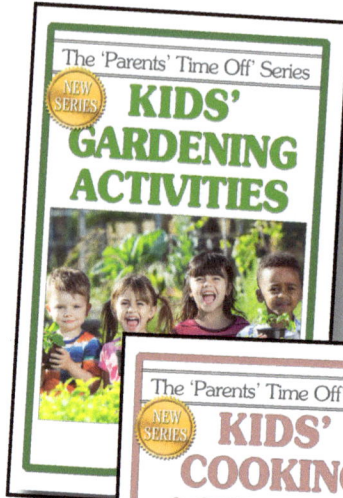

The 'Parents' Time Off' Series

NEW SERIES

KIDS'
GARDENING
ACTIVITIES

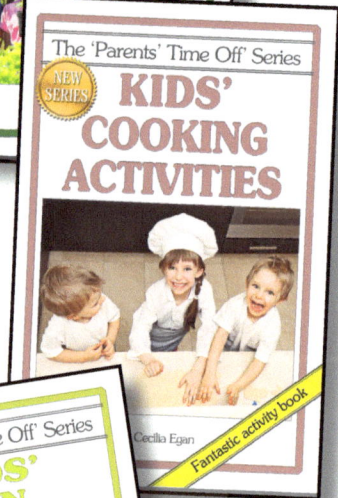

The 'Parents' Time Off' Series

NEW SERIES

KIDS'
COOKING
ACTIVITIES

Cecilia Egan

Fantastic activity book

The 'Parents' Time Off' Series

NEW SERIES

KIDS'
HANDS-ON
CRAFT
ACTIVITIES

Cecilia Egan

Fantastic activity book

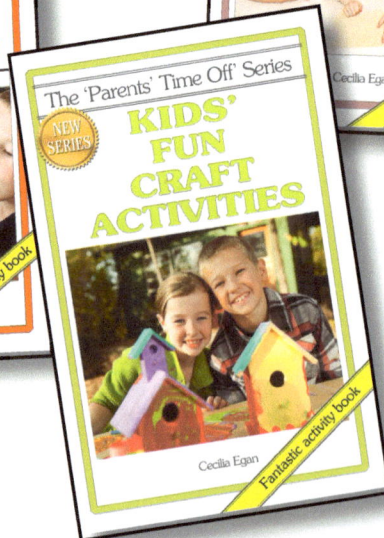

The 'Parents' Time Off' Series

NEW SERIES

KIDS'
FUN
CRAFT
ACTIVITIES

Cecilia Egan

Fantastic activity book

Fantastic activity books — no more school holiday boredom!

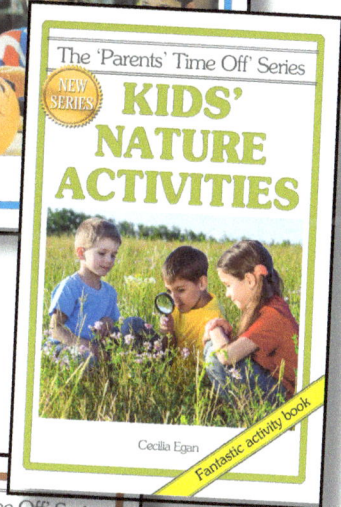

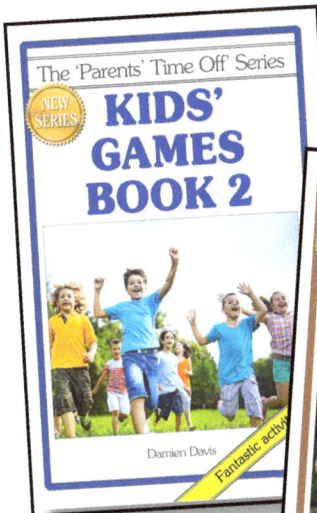

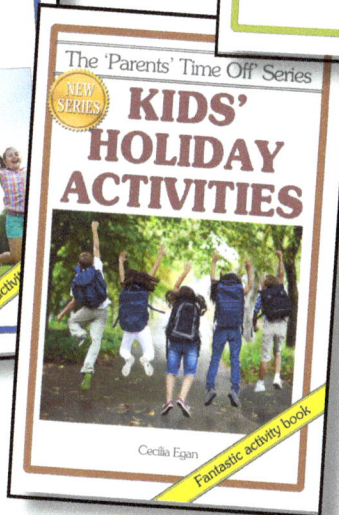

The 'Parents' Time Off' Series
NEW SERIES
KIDS' CREATIVE CRAFT ACTIVITIES
Cecilia Egan
Fantastic activity book

The 'Parents' Time Off' Series
NEW SERIES
KIDS' GAMES BOOK 1

The 'Parents' Time Off' Series
NEW SERIES
KIDS' NATURE ACTIVITIES
Cecilia Egan
Fantastic activity book

The 'Parents' Time Off' Series
NEW SERIES
KIDS' GAMES BOOK 2
Damien Davis
Fantastic activity

The 'Parents' Time Off' Series
NEW SERIES
KIDS' HOLIDAY ACTIVITIES
Cecilia Egan
Fantastic activity book

Princess Pam
Fell Into the Jam

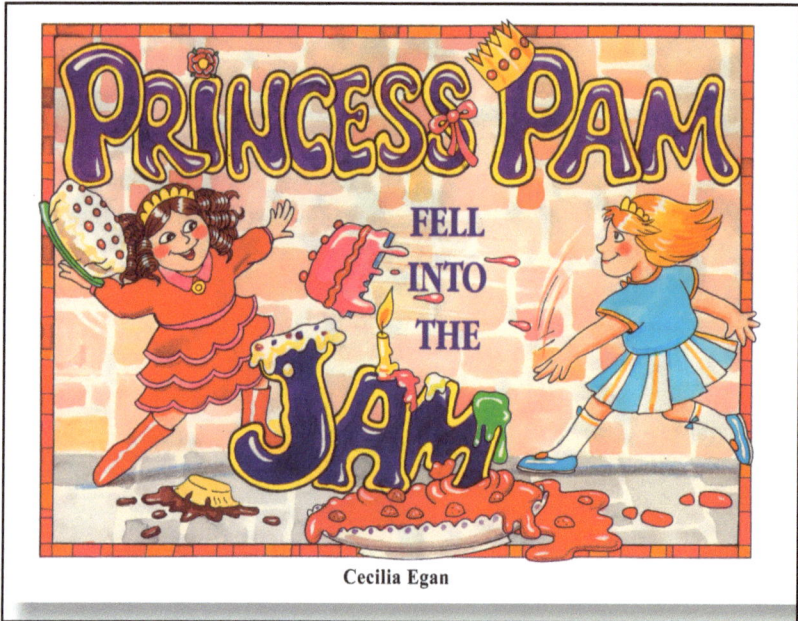

More than a hilarious rhyme, this is a slapstick comedy that causes a riot of laughter when read aloud. Princess Pam and her messy sisters appeal to every child.

The rollicking rhymes, the unconventional story and the lively, detailed pictures combine to make one of the funniest and most original children's books published.

Princess Pam
and the Twenty-eight Brave Princes

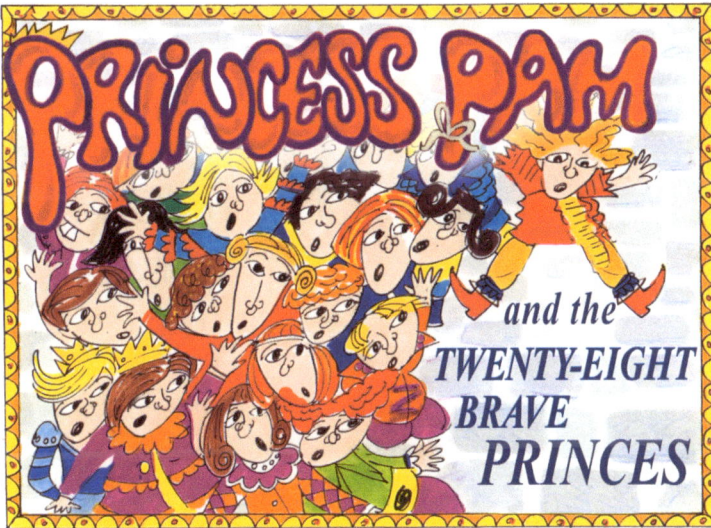

Cecilia Egan

In this, the second in the riotous "Princess Pam" series, Princess Pam becomes involved in more uproarious, slapstick comedy when she and her naughty sisters and cousins meet the Brave Princes.

Classic Fairytales from Tolkien's Bookshelf

- Grimms' Fairytales - Illustrated

- The Red Fairy Book - Illustrated

- The Princess and the Goblin - Illustrated.

- The Story of King Arthur and his Knights - Illustrated

Find out more on our website!

www.leavesofgoldpress.com

The Fairytale Sequels

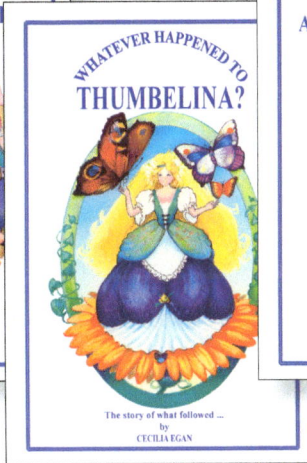

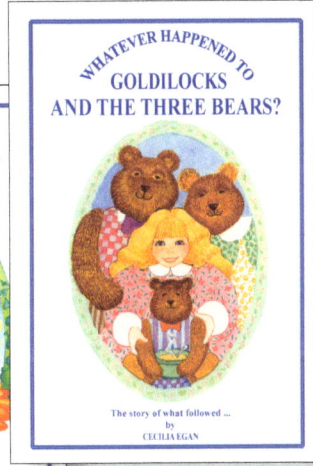

WHATEVER HAPPENED TO
THE THREE LITTLE P[...]

The story of what followed ...
by
CECILIA EGAN

WHATEVER HAPPENED TO
THUMBELINA?

The story of what followed ...
by
CECILIA EGAN

WHATEVER HAPPENED TO
GOLDILOCKS
AND THE THREE BEARS?

The story of what followed ...
by
CECILIA EGAN

The Nursery Rhyme Stories

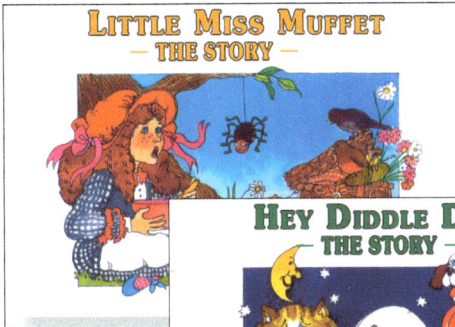

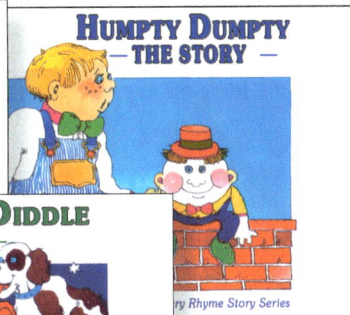

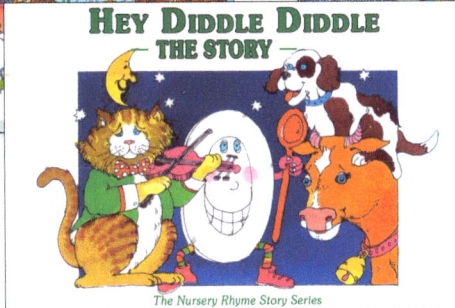

LITTLE MISS MUFFET
— THE STORY —

HUMPTY DUMPTY
— THE STORY —

...ry Rhyme Story Series

HEY DIDDLE DIDDLE
— THE STORY —

The Nursery Rhyme Story Series